No Longer Running

Keith Noel

Exploring Memory, Finding Meaning was a special project of the Adult Basic Education Writing Network. The Network gratefully acknowledges the financial support of the National Literacy Secretariat, Human Resources Development Canada.

Canadian Cataloguing in Publication Data

Noel, Keith, 1962-
    No longer running

(Exploring memory, finding meaning)
ISBN 0-9681338-5-1

    1. Readers for new literates. 2. Newfoundland–
Biography. I. Title. II. Series.

PE1126.N43N63 2000   428.6'2   C00-901047-5

Cover photograph: Marty Reeves

Design: C. Anne MacLeod

Published by:

HARRISH PRESS
18 Leslie St.
St. John's, NF
A1E 2V6
Phone 709-753-8815   Fax 709-753-8856
edplan@firstcity.net

To my father John Noel and
his wife Gertie

Contents

Foreword

This is one of a series of four books. They all began in a workshop where writers shared ideas and life stories, as well as thoughts about the fears and joys of writing itself. During the workshop, writers used photographs of people and places as doorways to the past, as ways to get at their memories and the stories that are important to them. Writers wrote about whatever the photographs brought to mind, then read their drafts aloud. Other writers and workshop leaders gave comments and asked questions. Then the writers went home to face the winter and the work of rewriting alone. Like most writing, this book is a product of both community and solitary work.

Keith Noel's *No Longer Running* is the story of how one man learns that he cannot run away from his problems. He travels from Newfoundland to Alberta and finds himself facing old fears in a new setting. Working in a park in the Rocky Mountains, he finds that nature and its beauty help and inspire him. But he feels he must go back home to face the past and to fulfill his dream of finishing his education. His story has lots of hard times and heartbreak. But as you read this writer's words, you'll get to know someone who faces life with courage and a sense of wonder–and always, with a sense of humour. He is a writer whose eyes are wide open to the world, to its joys and sorrows and comic details.

Between Hell and Heaven

This is my story of hell–and of coming back from it. It all began at the age of twenty-one when I took my first drink. That day I knew I already had a problem. I guess nobody really knows how close to hell we really are. I sometimes felt like I was standing halfway between hell and heaven.

Sometimes we try to forget a problem rather than deal with it. Alcohol brought nothing but pain to me and everyone I knew. It turned me into a person I didn't know. I began to get into a lot of trouble. Almost every time I went drinking, I drove my car and ended up in jail. And I still didn't think I had a problem. Or I pretended I didn't have a problem.

Time drifted by, and so did my alcohol problem. Underneath the alcohol, I was suffering from depression. The more I drank, the more depressed I became. My depression began to take my life. I felt I was going nowhere. My blood began to run cold but I didn't know how to deal with it. I tried to take the easy way out, to end it all. I couldn't even do that right. Or it wasn't my time to go. No matter how many pills I took, I still woke up every time. One time I took so many sleeping pills they probably would have killed a horse. I woke up three days later.

Nothing I tried seemed to work. By now, everybody I knew had begun to drift farther and farther away from me. I also began to withdraw from everyone. I soon forgot to try to reach out. Alone, I thought about my problem a lot, and tried to understand it. Maybe help was the answer. My doctor decided to put me in hospital. I spent thirty days on the third floor. It didn't seem too bad.

When I got out I thought: now, how do I keep my head together and stay clean? But I knew deep inside it was a matter of time and my problem would be back. I still didn't know how to deal with my depression, and that was going to be the real challenge. Every time I got depressed, I ran back to drinking. Nothing I tried worked.

Almost two and a half years after I left the hospital, it came back–first the depression and then the alcohol. This time it was ten times worse. Now I fell right back where I was before–on the road to hell. I became unpredictable. When I drank, I had no feeling or sense of life. I didn't give a damn about anyone or anything. It was only a matter of time, and I'd be right back in jail again.

I had to make a change in a hurry. Everybody I had once known had turned and walked away. You get used to people going away. At least you find out they were never friends to begin with. I learned to be alone and I still like it; the only person I need to trust today is myself. I know people can be insincere because I'm one of them. When a person has been let down as many times as I have, you just get sick of it all. You get to the point you don't need any friends.

But deep in my soul there was a burning fire, a fire that made me wander every time I got drunk. I'd drive my car even when I couldn't get out without falling on my face. I knew things had to change, and that's when I decided to go out west.

Go west, young man.

Go West, Young Man

It was October, 1991. Everybody was talking about all the jobs in the province of Alberta. I thought maybe if I moved to Alberta, my life might change. I made a phone call to my mother who lived there to ask if she would mind if I stayed with her for two months. She said it was okay. So I managed to get enough money for a plane ticket to Calgary and began to make arrangements.

I'll never forget the day I left St. John's. Looking out the window, I could see my father's car in the parking lot. It was the first time I'd seen my father in a very long time. It was nice to know he came to watch me fly away. I felt my heart rip, hoping I had made the right decision.

As the plane taxied down the runway, the winds were gusting up to seventy miles per hour and I could feel the plane sway back and forth.

Then the engines roared as the plane lifted off. A feeling of loneliness came over me. I felt cold inside as the plane climbed higher and higher. It didn't take very long to get above the clouds. But I wasn't thinking about the sky. It was my first time on a plane, and it was just my luck to get a window seat. From the time I left, I was dying to go to the bathroom. But the two women who sat next to me were so slow to move that I was almost in Calgary before I got to go.

When I glanced out the window, I saw the biggest checkerboard I'd ever seen. The land was multicolored squares. It looked real cool. Then the plane began its descent. I couldn't wait to put my feet back on the ground again. I hoped my mother would be there to pick me up. The plane bounced two or three times and we were on the runway. *It won't be long now and I'll be in the terminal and out of this tin can*, I thought. *At least now I know how it feels to be a can of beans.*

As the plane docked at the terminal I felt relaxed. I felt excited to be somewhere I'd never been before. This place was so big compared to the St. John's airport. It had a lot of nice displays, stuffed animals; everything looked so cool.

I was hoping my mother hadn't forgotten me. Sometimes I can be just like a kid. I wandered off, forgetting to look for her. I must have been walking around the terminal for close to an hour when I finally spotted her by the luggage pickup area. I could see that she was happy to see me. She ran towards me with her arms spread out like a plane's wings. For a second I thought she was drunk, and then she gave me a big hug. The first thing that came to my mind was, *people are going to think I'm mommy's little boy. How embarrassing!* I have always found it hard to deal with my feelings.

My blood was still running cold but it was good to be in a new environment. The sun was shining; it was going to be a good day for the drive from Calgary to Canmore. We picked up my luggage, headed to the car, put the luggage in the trunk and drove off. As we were leaving the airport, I could see the Rocky Mountains in the distance. They were just like what I'd seen on TV. The peaks were covered with snow. It was October 29. The winter would not be long coming, but for now I'd enjoy the weather.

The mountains reached up to the sky.

Reaching Up to the Sky

We turned onto the Trans-Canada Highway west to Canmore. As the miles rolled up on the odometer, the car rolled up to the mountains. I'd never seen anything so beautiful in my life. The mountains reached up to the sky like they were trying to tell me something. It was like what I was trying to do, but they where already there.

I began to read the highway signs. The communities had names like Bragg Creek, Cochrane, then Morley, and Stony Indian Reservation. It was the first time I'd ever seen houses so far apart. Exshaw was the next town. It was very small. I guessed from looking at all the industrial plants that Exshaw must be a working town. It took maybe five minutes to drive through Exshaw. We were fifteen minutes from Canmore.

I just couldn't get over the scenery.

Canmore wasn't very big either. It was surrounded by mountains. I thought that the sun must not shine very long in Canmore. The high mountains kept it out, and they made a person feel small.

That night at the hotel, my mother and I talked about where we could go tomorrow. We decided to spend the day at Radium Hot Springs. After a good sleep, we were up and on our way. I just couldn't get over the scenery as we drove through the Rocky Mountains. We made a detour to see Lake Louise. It was just like a picture you often see on a calendar. We didn't stay long, just long enough to see everything we could. Then we were back on the road to Radium. We made a pit stop at Golden for something to eat.

I had not known there were so many little towns in the Mountains. Every little town we drove through made me wonder why people settled there. I knew I would love to live here. It seemed to me the kind of place where it would be easy for a person to forget all their problems.

We headed down Highway 95. I thought to

My moustache was covered in ice.

myself, *nothing can get any better than this.* Then, as we pulled into the parking lot at Radium, I had one look and thought everybody was gone nuts. It was enough to freeze... Well, you get the idea. It was at least -10 degrees out. In we walked to get our tickets so we could look like nuts too. My body went into shock as I walked to the pool. But the pool itself was like a hot tub. I might have looked like a nut, but who cares? This was great. I was in the pool for maybe five minutes, and my moustache was covered in ice and my bald head was numb from the cold.

I met new people and had fun.

247 Cords of Firewood Later

We toured around Alberta for a week or so. Then it was time to start looking for work. It didn't take me very long to find a job with the Bow Valley Provincial Park. Mike, my boss, gave me the details about the job. I'd be cutting firewood for all the campgrounds in the Bow Valley and Kananaskis. That winter our crew cut 247 cords of firewood.

It was hard work and I just loved it. Working outdoors was great. But all the firewood we cut that winter didn't last very long. By the end of the summer it was almost gone. I'll never forget that winter. I met new people and had fun. I ended up working in the Bow Valley Park for more than three years.

I was transferred to Kananaskis Village. There were three hotels there. My job there would be to cut grass in the summer and plow snow in the winter. My time was getting short. All the parks jobs were out for tender. I just tried to forget it and do my job. It seemed to me that everything was going great. The summer was almost over, the trees were losing their leaves to the earth, and the wind began to get cold. When the snow began to fall, my job got pretty neat. I don't think I have ever seen so much snow fall in one day. It just kept coming and I kept plowing.

Losses and Learning

I tried not to think about losing my job, but there were other losses to think about. It was sometime after that winter that the man who gave me the job took his own life. Sometimes this comes to my mind, bringing back so many memories I try to forget.

The next year I lost the girl I was going to marry. Too much pressure had begun to build up. By now all the parks were privately owned. So I moved to Edmonton where I started a job in a garage.

Edmonton was a very big city. After I settled into my new job, I decided to go the West Edmonton Mall. I couldn't believe how big it was. It was the first time I had ever seen so many things in one place.

I toured around Edmonton for awhile, and got to see all the beautiful scenery. Slowly my life began to fall into place. I think I finally found out what I wanted from life. It was something I'd never had–an education.

I'd had enough of hell, and enough of running. I did not want to race anymore, or reach up like the mountains. I quit my job. I had only one thing on my mind. I was going home, back to St. John's to get an education. I had been home six months when I began to attend the Rabbittown Learners Program. I know for sure that it is making me a whole different person. I give thanks to Doris Hapgood, Greg Connors, Betty Gabriel, Lori Hapgood and Anita Fisher at Rabbittown; Michelle Park at the John Howard Society; and Dave Clarke, Department of Human Resources and Employment, for their support. They all have helped me get where I am today. People like these can really make a difference in someone's life.

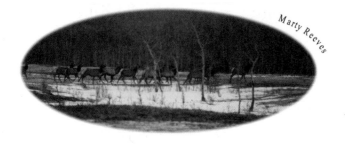

Marty Reeves

Acknowledgements

This book was developed for Exploring Memory, Finding Meaning, a special project of the Adult Basic Education Writing Network. We offer our thanks to the National Literacy Secretariat for their financial support of the book series.

We also thank those who helped with the photographs. Many were found in the author's photograph albums. We could not identify the source for all those images but we would like to thank Marty Reeves, whose photographs capture the spirit of the Rockies.

Participants and staff at the Rabbittown Learners Program in St. John's, the Learning Centre in Edmonton, and the Discovery Centre in Bay Roberts field tested earlier drafts of the books. Their comments and suggestions helped us improve the series.